# 10 Words

**FOR DAILY INSPIRATION, ENCOURAGEMENT & MOTIVATION**

Eleanor Curry

**Gotham Books**

30 N Gould St.
Ste. 20820, Sheridan, WY 82801
https://gothambooksinc.com/

Phone: 1 (307) 464-7800

© 2023 Eleanor Curry. All rights reserved.

No part of this book may be reproduced, stored in a retrieval system, or transmitted by any means without the written permission of the author.

Published by Gotham Books (December 27, 2023)

ISBN: 979-8-88775-503-8 (P)
ISBN: 979-8-88775-504-5 (E)

Because of the dynamic nature of the Internet, any web addresses or links contained in this book may have changed since publication and may no longer be valid.

The views expressed in this work are solely those of the author and do not necessarily reflect the views of the publisher, and the publisher hereby disclaims any responsibility for them.

ften times we become so busy in our daily routines that it can become overwhelming at times. As you grow older and mature in Christ you begin to appreciate the things that really matter most a lot less of yourself and more of God.

Some things happen or occur in life to open our eyes a little wider so that you can see more clearly and understand that God is teaching us to call on him and trust in him and to assure you that you are not alone. As for myself I have always tried to go the extra mile to make people like me or fit in worried about what people thought or think about me.

Now all that matters is what God thinks about me. I am only trying to please the Lord at this point in my life and become a better woman of God and let the Lord use me and live by his word and stay in his will. There are so many distractions that may come your way when you make up in your mind to serve the Lord with your whole heart, mind, body and soul.

I use to allow stress to consume me until I got to the point that one day, I realized that enough is enough I am a child of the most high God. I am humbled and thankful and I will not go a day without laughter. It is so important life can really tear you down if you let it remain strong in the Lord and obey his law. So that you can lead others to the kingdom of God. Learn several scriptures to meditate on every day to make your day better and to improve your journey.

Leave your past and your old ways, habits, attitudes and excuses behind. We must not blame others for your mistakes and the choices that we made in life. Learn from them and leave them behind so that you can move forward.

Forgive others and everyone that may have harmed or hurt you, let it go so that you can move on with your life don't stay stuck in the same mess or thoughts release it, release it, release it let go and let God. For if ye forgive men their trespasses, your heavenly Father will also forgive you: (Matthew 6:14) So that you can start to enjoy life and get excited about your future and what's to come and living life to the fullest.

Forgive yourself stop blaming yourself for the should've, could've, or if I only had done things differently things would be different, accept the things that happened and move forward ask the Lord for forgiveness and repent for your mistakes and move forward.

As I allowed the Lord to work things out issues that troubled me the most became smaller, as I became focused and spent more time with the Lord in prayer and reading my bible more with all my getting, I got understanding and became wiser. When you surrender all the Lord will work it out and give you a peace that surpasses all understanding.

As I look back over my life and I think things over, I can truly say that I've been blessed, I have a testimony. The Lord is so awesome and amazing. Give the Lord a chance to love, change and comfort you. He is worth every minute.

When I allowed the Lord to take control of my life, I was able to receive my deliverance and healing there is no love like God's love.

It is impossible to love another person, if don't love yourself you first must love yourself once you learn to love yourself and only then can you show love and share God's love.

Let your light so shine through me Lord, use me to glorify your name and spread your word to help others, know that any obstacle can be overcome and you are more than a conqueror through.

Jesus Christ share, give and receive love there are no limits when you serve and love the Lord and live by his word.

I just wanted to share some very vital points and display some quick references from the Bible for daily meditation when you are on the go or when you need some encouragement. Just a friendly reminder to laugh when you feel sad, abide in God's law, lead others to the Lord, learn the word of God, leave your past behind, live life to the fullest, let the Lord's light shine through you, live a holy lifestyle, love yourself so that you can love others, trust in the lord with your whole heart and lean not to your own understanding and he shall direct your path.

# Contents

Laugh (Joy) .................................................................. 1

Law ............................................................................. 2

Lead ............................................................................ 3

Learn .......................................................................... 4

Leave .......................................................................... 5

Life ............................................................................. 6

Light ........................................................................... 7

Live ............................................................................ 8

Love ........................................................................... 9

Lord .......................................................................... 10

# Laugh (Joy)

For this day is holy unto our Lord: neither be ye sorry; for the joy of the Lord is your strength.

**NEHEMIAH (8:10) KJV**

For his anger endureth but a moment; in his favour is life: weeping may endure for a night, but joy cometh in the morning.

**PSALM (30:5) KJV**

Restore unto me the joy of thy salvation; and uphold me with thy free spirit.

**PSALM (51:12) KJV**

Make a joyful noise unto God, all ye lands:

**PSALM (66:1) KJV**

I say unto you, that likewise joy shall be in heaven over one sinner that repenteth, more than over ninety and nine just persons, which need no repentance.

**LUKE (15:7) KJV**

# *Law*

I have longed for thy salvation, O Lord; and thy law is my delight.

**PSALM (119:174) KJV**

For what the law could not do, in that it was weak through the flesh, God sending his own Son in the likeness of sinful flesh, and for sin, condemned sin in the flesh:

That the righteousness of the law might be fulfilled in us, who walk not after the flesh, but after the Spirit.

**ROMANS (8:3,4) KJV**

For all the law is fulfilled in one word, even in this; thou shalt love thy neighbor as thyself.

**GALATIANS (5:14) KJV**

But whoso looketh into the perfect law of liberty, and continueth therein, he being not a forgetful hearer, but a doer of the work, this man shall be blessed in his deed.

**JAMES (1:25) KJV**

# Lead

He maketh me to lie down in green pastures: he <u>lead</u>eth me beside the still waters. He restoreth my soul: he <u>lead</u>eth me in the paths of righteousness for his name's sake.

**PSALM (23:2,3) KJV**

And see if there be any wicked way in me, and <u>lead</u> me in the way everlasting.

**PSALM (139:24) KJV**

And <u>lead</u> us not into temptation, but deliver us from evil: For thine is the kingdom, and the power, and the glory, forever. A-men'.

**MATTHEW (6:13) KJV**

For kings, and for all that are in authority; that we may <u>lead</u> a quiet and peaceable life in all godliness and honesty.

For this is good and acceptable in the sight of God our Savior;

**1 TIMOTHY (2:2,3) KJV**

# Learn

A wise man will hear, and will increase learning; and a man of understanding shall attain unto wise counsels:

**PROVERBS (1:5) KJV**

Give instruction to a wise man, and he will be yet wiser: teach a just man, and he will increase in learning.

**PROVERBS (9:9) KJV**

The wise in heart shall be called prudent: and the sweetness of the lips increaseth learning.

**PROVERBS (16:21) KJV**

The heart of the wise teacheth his mouth, and addeth learning to his lips.

**PROVERBS (16:23) KJV**

Take my yoke upon you, and learn of me; for I am meek and lowly in heart: and ye shall find rest unto your souls.

**MATTHEW (11:29) KJV**

# *Leave*

And he answered and said unto them, have ye not read, that he which made them at the beginning made them male and female, and said, for this cause shall a man <u>leave</u> father and mother and shall cleave to his wife: and they twain shall be one flesh?

**MATTHEW (19:4,5) KJV**


Peace I <u>leave</u> with you, my peace I give unto you: not as the world giveth, give I unto you. Let not your heart be troubled, neither let it be afraid.

**JOHN (14:27) KJV**


Let your conversation be without covetousness; and be content with such things as ye have: for he hath said. I will never <u>leave</u> thee, nor forsake thee.

**HEBREWS (13:5) KJV**

# Life

For whose findeth me findeth <u>life</u>, and shall obtain favour of the Lord.

**PROVERBS (8:35) KJV**

Verily, verily I say unto you, He that heareth my word, and believeth on him that sent me, hath everlasting <u>life</u>, and shall not come into condemnation; but is passed from death unto life.

**JOHN (5:24) KJV**

Jesus saith unto him, I am the way, the truth, and the <u>life</u>: no man cometh unto the father, but by me.

**JOHN (14:6) KJV**

I am crucified with Christ: nevertheless, I live; yet not I, but Christ Liveth in me: and the <u>life</u> which I now live in the flesh I live by the faith of the Son of God, who loved me, and gave himself for me.

**GALATIANS (2:20) KJV**

# *Light*

Thy word is a lamp unto my feet, and a light unto my path.

**PSALM (119:105) KJV**

Let your <u>light</u> so shine before men, that they may see your good works, and glorify your Father which is in heaven.

**MATTHEW (5:16) KJV**

But if we walk in the <u>light</u>, as he is in the light, we have fellowship one with another, and the blood of Jesus Christ his Son cleanseth us from all sin.

**1 JOHN (1:7) KJV**

And there shall be no night there; and they need no candle, neither light of the sun; for the Lord God giveth them <u>light</u>: and they shall reign for ever and ever.

**REVELATIONS (22:5) KJV**

# *Live*

But he answered and said, it is written, man shall not <u>live</u> by bread alone, but by every word that procedeeth out of the mouth of God.

**MATTHEW (4:4) KJV**

For in him we <u>live</u>, and move, and have our being; as certain also of your own poets have said, for we are also his offspring.

**ACTS (17:28) KJV**

For therein is the righteousness of God revealed from faith to faith: as it is written, the just shall <u>live</u> by faith.

**ROMANS (1:17) KJV**

If we <u>live</u> in the Spirit, let us also walk in the Spirit.

**GALATIANS (5:25) KJV**

# Love

And thou shalt <u>love</u> the Lord thy God with all thine heart, and with all thy soul, and with all thy might.

**DEUTERONOMY (6:5) KJV**

But I say unto you, <u>love</u> your enemies, bless them that curse you, do good to them that hate you, and pray for them which despitefully use you, and persecute you;

**MATTHEW (5:44) KJV**

This is my commandment, that ye <u>love</u> one another, as I have loved you.

**JOHN (15:12) KJV**

We <u>love</u> him, because he first loved us.

**1 JOHN (4:19) KJV**

# Lord

Praise the Lord with harp: sing unto him with the psaltery and an instrument of ten strings.

**PSALM (33:2) KJV**

Not everyone that saith unto me, Lord, Lord, shall enter into the kingdom of heaven; but he that doeth the will of my Father which is in Heaven.

**MATTHEW (7:21) KJV**

One Lord, one faith, one baptism, One God and Father of all, who is above all, and through all, and in you all.

**EPHESIANS (4:5,6) KJV**

Now the Lord of peace himself give you peace always by all means. The Lord be with you all.

**2 THESSALONIANS (3:16) KJV**